# The Collector's Encyclopedia of

# OCCUPIED JAPAN

## Collectibles

By

**Gene Florence**

**COLLECTOR BOOKS**

*A Division of Schroeder Publishing Co., Inc.*

The current values in this book should be used only as a guide. They are not intended to set prices, which vary from one section of the country to another. Auction prices as well as dealer prices vary greatly and are affected by condition as well as demand. Neither the Author nor the Publisher assumes responsibility for any losses that might be incurred as a result of consulting this guide.

Additional copies of this book may be ordered from:

COLLECTOR BOOKS
P.O. Box 3009
Paducah, Kentucky 42001
or
Gene Florence
P.O. Box 22186
Lexington, Kentucky 40522

@ $14.95 Add $2.00 for postage and handling.
Copyright: Bill Schroeder, Gene Florence, 1976
Values Updated 1990

# FOREWORD

The collecting of "Occupied Japan" has mushroomed in the last few years. The objects marked with these magic words are readily found and are of surprising variety. To understand the why of collecting things from this particular time period is not one of the major purposes of this book; it may be that it, like the mountain, is "there"; but a little background information may be helpful.

All items made in Japan, from the beginning of our occupation at the end of World War II until April 28, 1952, when the occupation ended, that were to be exported to the United States had to be marked in one of four ways: "Japan," "Made in Japan," "Occupied Japan" or "Made in Occupied Japan." You can tell that, if all markings were even used equally, only half of the items exported during this time period would now be considered collectible. Due to the fact that many Japanese were not overjoyed with the occupation to begin with, it's not too unrealistic to assume that far fewer than half of the items were marked to advertise the fact. In any case, you will find many similar or even like items which will offer only "Japan" or "Made in Japan," and thus there is little way of actually proving that the piece was made during the period of Occupation. When something is made in a limited number or over a limited time, someone is bound to begin collecting it. This has happened with the items exported with the words "Made in Occupied Japan" stamped on them. The collecting which started quietly at first is now taking voice and being heard throughout the land.

This book will offer you a sample of the objects made; and, even with over one thousand three hundred items shown, you will be able to find numerous items which aren't represented. Basically, this is a beginning, with the collectible objects being broken into working categories for both new and advanced collectors alike.

By far the most prevalent of all "Occupied Japan" items are the figurines to which only two-fifths of this book is devoted. Since the figurines are so plentiful when compared to other things available, many collectors are concentrating on other types of objects. On the other hand, there are collectors who collect only the figurines. Whichever you prefer, I believe you will find adequate examples to whet your collecting appetite.

There is no substitute for quality; so, if you pick a category such as figurines, don't settle for all you can find —unless the price is unbelievably cheap! Rather, pick the pieces that are well-made and decorated nicely. Over a period of time, quality items maintain their value and collectibility far more than do the cheaper, inferiorly made ones.

# PRICING

All prices in this book are retail prices. The prices you see here are based upon what I have found "Occupied Japan" items selling for today. They are not "wishful" prices. Nearly all the items in the book have been purchased in the last year so that current market prices are reflected. I am aware of the fact that you can buy other books on "Occupied Japan" with prices two to five times as high as I have listed. Again, I have tried to price items realistically. If you buy something listed for $75.00 in one book for the "bargain" price of $50.00 and then can't sell it for more than $10.00, you should recognize why, in my book, it only lists for $10.00 in the first place.

Again, all prices in this book are retail prices—what the piece is actually selling for. If you sell to a dealer, however, you can expect up to fifty percent off the retail price. Better quality and more expensive items may bring up to eighty percent of the prices listed; but, on the more common items, you will be lucky to average fifty percent. It's a hard, cruel fact, but, with overhead and time considered into prices, many dealers operate at poverty levels as it is. Ask the previous owners of many shops which have gone out of business in the last few years. Still, if you have a piece stored in the attic that you bought twenty years ago for 50¢ and a dealer will give you $2.50 for it now, that's not bad profit—and it hasn't eaten anything over all those years!

Damaged pieces, unless they are extremely scarce items, have little value to most collectors; therefore, all prices listed herein are for perfect (mint) condition pieces.

Too, unlike the Depression Glass book, which stated categorically that this piece in this pattern was worth this much money, the prices here are to be taken generally. I don't mean for you to look at a piece and try to find the price for that EXACT piece. Of the billions of pieces exported, only about one thousand, three hundred are represented here. They're here to give you the GENERAL IDEA of what a piece of about this size and workmanship are worth so that, when you come across something you like, you'll at least know if the price is "in the ball park" or not.

## WARNING

In the past few months some unscrupulous persons have been faking "Occupied Japan" items by using a rubber stamp to mark the pieces. If you are suspicious of a mark on any glazed item, use finger nail polish remover or a similar substance on the mark. It will not disappear if it is the original version since these marks are under the glaze.

# TABLE OF CONTENTS

Animals ........................................................... 8-11
Ash Trays—Ceramic ......................................... 12-13
Ash Trays (Metal) and Metallic Objects ............. 14-15
Book Ends, Bud Vases and Bric-A-Brac ............. 16-17
Canister Set ..................................................... 18-19
Celluloid .......................................................... 20-21
Children's Tea Sets .......................................... 22-23
Cup and Saucer Sets ........................................ 24-25
Decorative Items .............................................. 26-27
Dinnerware ...................................................... 28-29
Fish Bowl Items ............................................... 30-31
Glass Objects ................................................... 32-33
Lacquerware ..................................................... 34-35
Lamps .............................................................. 36-37
Lighters and Miscellaneous Metal Objects .......... 38-39
Novelty Items ................................................... 40-41
Paper and Wood Products ................................. 42-43
Planters (Primarly Animal) ............................... 44-45
Planters—People .............................................. 46-47
Salt and Pepper Shakers ................................... 48-51
Souvenir Items ................................................. 52-53
Tea Sets ........................................................... 54-57
Toby Mugs, Etc. ............................................... 58-59
Toothpicks and Bud Vases ................................ 60-61
Toys ................................................................. 62-63
Vases—Small ................................................... 64-65
Vases—Large ................................................... 66-67

## FIGURINES

Angels and Elves .............................................. 68-69
Bisque Figurines ............................................... 70-71
Bisque Pairs and Shelf Sitters ........................... 72-73
Children ........................................................... 74-75
Children Musicians ........................................... 76-77
Children Shelf Sitters, et al. ............................. 78-79
Dancing Girls ................................................... 80-81
Dancing Pairs ................................................... 82-83
Delft Blue Figurines .......................................... 84-85
Figurine Couples and Groups ............................ 86-87
Musicians ......................................................... 88-89
Orientals .......................................................... 90-91
Oriental Pairs ................................................... 92-93
Pairs of Figurines ............................................. 94-95
Sets and Partial Sets ........................................ 96-97
Statues, Statues and More Statues .................... 98-103
Symbolic Figurines ........................................... 104-105
Unbelievable Ending ......................................... 106-107

# ACKNOWLEDGMENTS

The behind the scenes story of a book is probably as interesting as the book itself; but the rewrites, giggles, irritations and Freudian slips for this one are history now and too many to enumerate. I will say that I'm sure my publisher wondered if this book would ever be finished during his lifetime! At times, I wondered if it would make it in mine—especially after we decided to move from one house to another "midstream," so to speak!

Several people have generously loaned me their "Occupied Japan" treasures and I would like to thank them all but, particularly, John and Trannie Davis of Acworth, Ga.; Mel and Claudia Steuben of Arlington, Va.; Mrs. Harold Rhoads of Lexington, Ky.; and Mr. and Mrs. William Mills of Dry Ridge, Ky. I especially need to thank my Mom for the use of her shakers; my Dad for hunting through Lexington's junk shops for me; my sister, Lois, for her prized pieces and proofing time; and my wife, Cathy, who served as typist, editor, critic and packing and re-wrap clerk at the photographing session.

Thank you, readers. I sincerely hope you enjoy it—and profit from it!

# The Collector's Encyclopedia of

# OCCUPIED JAPAN

## Collectibles

# ANIMALS

Animals constitute one of the more collectible areas of "Occupied Japan (ese)" objects. Some collectors specialize in only one type of animal, i.e., dogs, cats, frogs. Some collect any type of animal. This particular field of interest seems to have an infinite variety of species, shapes, antics and expression. Should you decide to collect in this realm of "Occupied Japan," I doubt that you'd have to worry about repetition of an object. Of the animals shown here and on the following page, I'm rather partial to Sir Turtle in row four, the very realistic butterflies and the utilitarian frogs.

Many animals come in sets, or even "teams," as shown on the next page by the musician bees, the duckling duet, and the baseball playing bears.

Sizes of the objects here range from 1½ inches to 4 inches high.

| | |
|---|---|
| *Top Row:* | |
| Dogs | $ 3.50- 4.50 |
| Pigs | 5.50- 6.50 |
| Lady Bugs | 8.50-10.00 |
| Ducks | 3.50- 3.75 |
| *2nd Row:* | |
| Dogs | 7.00- 8.50 |
| Bird | 3.50- 4.00 |
| Receiving Set | 3.50- 4.50 |
| *3rd Row:* | |
| Dogs | 9.00-10.00 |
| Deer | 4.00- 4.50 |
| Duck | 6.00- 6.50 |
| Bird | 3.50- 3.75 |
| *4th Row:* | |
| Dogs | 8.00- 9.50 |
| Birds | 3.00- 3.50 |
| Lamb | 2.50- 3.00 |
| Turtle | 8.00-10.00 |
| Bee | 7.50- 8.00 |
| *5th Row:* | |
| Dogs | 17.50-20.00 |

# ANIMALS (con't)

*Top Row:*

| | |
|---|---|
| Bears | $7.00- 7.50 ea. |
| Dogs | 5.00- 6.00 |
| Monkey Set | 4.50- 5.00 |

*2nd Row:*

| | |
|---|---|
| Dog | 7.00- 7.50 |
| (same dog as in top row, only larger) | |
| Horse | 6.00- 7.50 |
| Pig | 5.00- 5.50 |
| Peacocks | 5.00- 6.00 |
| Mouse | 6.50- 7.00 |

*3rd Row:*

| | |
|---|---|
| Cat | 4.00- 4.50 |
| Cat Groups | 8.00-10.00 |
| Butterflies | 7.50- 8.50 |
| Dog | 3.00- 3.50 |

*4th Row:*

| | |
|---|---|
| Cats | 5.00- 5.50 |
| Horse Drawn Planter | 5.00- 6.00 |
| Ox Drawn Planter | 4.50- 5.00 |
| Dogs | 6.00- 6.50 |

*5th Row:*

| | |
|---|---|
| Frog Ash Tray | 10.00-12.50 |
| Frog Vase | 12.50-15.00 |
| Fish | 3.00- 3.50 |
| Peacock | 5.00- 6.50 |
| Cat Pencil Holder | 3.00- 3.50 |

# ASH TRAYS—Ceramic

Here is but a sampling of the host of ash trays which exist; yet, I'm pleased with the diversity of this small lot. Particularly note the alligator! Isn't he an attention getter!

Many ash trays come as sets such as the brown elephant one shown at the top of the photo. Too, the cigarette boxes shown each have matching ash trays which may either stack beside the box or in it when not in use.

The "Wedgewood"-like ash trays in the second row are decorative but not of comparable quality to the English china it obviously tries to emulate.

Some of these ash trays may not be the most decorative or colorful of the "Occupied Japan" objects to be collected, but they surely must number among the most useful. Everyone needs an ash tray or two—even non-smokers have to occasionally accommodate the noxious habits of friends; so why not have them of collectible "Occupied Japan"? The really nice thing is that they aren't yet as expensive as some you'll find at the five and dime store.

*Top Row:*
  Coal Bin and Tray                                    $17.50-20.00
  Elephant Set (5 Trays)                                17.50-20.00
*2nd Row:*
  Alligator                                             11.00-12.50
  "Wedgewood" Types                                      7.50- 8.50
  Frog                                                  10.00-12.50
*3rd Row:*
  Dresser and Top                                        6.00- 6.50
  Cigarette Boxes (4 Trays)                             17.50-22.50
*4th Row:*
  Cigarette Box (4 Trays)                               15.00-17.50
  Ash Trays (Part of Sets Above)                         2.50- 3.00
*Bottom:*
  Square Ash Tray                                        2.00- 2.50
  Rose Ash Tray                                          2.50- 3.00 ea.
  /Set of 4 and Box.                                    17.50-20.00
  Negro Holder                                          17.50-20.00
  Queen of Hearts, Part of Set                           3.00- 3.50 ea.
  Oriental Face, Part of Set                             3.00- 3.50
  /Set w/box                                            17.50-20.00
  Leaf                                                   3.00- 3.50
  Rectangular Tray                                       3.00- 3.50

# ASH TRAYS (Metal) and METALLIC OBJECTS

White metal (antimony) objects, especially ash trays, are among the least often recognized "Occupied Japan" items. People who will turn over every piece on a table and check the marking on the bottom will pass right over metallic "Occupied Japan."

My favorite of the metal pieces shown here, naturally, is the coppery looking ash tray with the galloping horses announcing it as a souvenir of Lexington, Kentucky, my home and birth place. Don't write me asking to buy it, please; your money just won't be any good. Yet, don't be discouraged. Wherever you call home, there is every likelihood of your being able to turn up a souvenir piece that's meaningful to you.

The rotating cable car is a nice kind of adult toy as well as an ash tray; and people of a certain bent might get a fiendish glee out of stubbing out their cigarettes in the face of the devil.

*Top Row:*
| | |
|---|---|
| Rotating Cable Car, San Francisco | $20.00-25.00 |
| Horses, Lexington, KY. | 5.00- 6.00 |

*2nd Row:*
| | |
|---|---|
| St. Louis Zoo | 2.50- 3.00 |
| Large Cowboy Tray | 3.00- 3.50 |
| Hollywood | 2.50- 3.00 |

*3rd Row:*
| | |
|---|---|
| Dog Cigarette or Jewel Box | 8.50- 9.50 |
| St. Petersburg, Fla. Tray | 2.50- 3.00 |
| Jewel Box | 6.00- 6.50 |
| Double Tray | 3.50- 4.50 |
| Cowboy Boot Lighter/Tray | 12.50-15.00 |

*4th Row:*
| | |
|---|---|
| Large Ash Tray | 4.50- 5.00 |
| Small Tray | 2.50- 3.00 |
| Devil Ash Tray | 12.50-15.00 |

Bottom:
| | |
|---|---|
| Silent Butler | 10.00-12.50 |
| Butter Dish (Glass Liner) | 10.00-12.50 |
| Florida Ash Tray | 2.50- 3.00 |
| Cigarette Box/Ash Tray on Stand | 15.00-17.50 |

# BOOKENDS, BUD VASES and BRIC-A-BRAC

There are only so many single classifications feasible in a book like this with such a multitudinous assortment of items; hence, the bric-a-brac. Well, under what heading would YOU put half a potty prominently labeled "for my half-ass friends"? Then there's the "Butt Snuffer," the pun being cheekily obvious, and the outhouse. Humor?

The little Dutch girl bell represents the only one I have seen marked "Occupied Japan," I have checked a number of others which were similar, but they either had no marking at all or merely "Made in Japan."

*Top Row:*
| | |
|---|---|
| Cream Pitcher (Part of Tea Set) | $9.00-10.00 |
| Egg Cup (Part of Dinnerware Set) | 12.50-15.00 |
| Pitcher | 4.50-5.00 |
| Half Potty | 3.00- 3.50 |

*2nd Row:*
| | |
|---|---|
| Book Ends | 20.00-25.00 |
| Pitcher | 7.50-10.00 |

*3rd Row:*
| | |
|---|---|
| Stacking Set (Missing One Part and Lid) | 3.00 ea./12.50 set |
| Black Boy at Outhouse | 22.50-25.00 |
| Cup and Saucer | 17.50-20.00 |
| Dutch Girl Bell | 12.50-15.00 |
| Candle Holder | 15.00 ea./30.00 pr |

*Bottom:*
| | |
|---|---|
| Cornucopia Vase | 4.50- 5.00 |
| Vase | 4.00- 4.50 |
| Covered Powder Jar | 8.00-10.00 |
| Butt Snuffer | 4.50- 5.00 |
| Pitcher | 3.50- 4.00 |
| Vase | 3.50- 4.00 |

# CANISTER SET

It is unusual these days to find a complete set of canisters if they were used at all. You may look long and hard. Thankfully, one of my Depression Glass friends had this set. Naturally, if you want a set, it will be easier to purchase it all at one time than trying to make one up piece by piece; but then, some people get a kick out of doing things the hard way; and, too, some people are fantastically lucky at doing just that sort of thing.

$20.00-25.00 each if sold separately

$125.00-150.00 set

# CELLULOID

First of all, there are two dolls in the photograph which are not celluloid, a faux pas; they're easily spotted and are "Occupied Japan," of course. The reindeer, alas, pre-"Rudolph," is part of a Christmas ensemble. The two baby rattles still perform said function though they have been somewhat "worked over."

Upon winding, the entwined couple will dance a kind of merry-go-round waltz and the Scottie dog shows immeasurable happiness by the vigorous movement of his tail. The little pig will measure up to a foot if you pull the ring in his nose.

The koochie koo dolls were prizes at amusement parks all over the country; few have survived; they weren't exactly the type you gave your little girl to play with anyway.

I don't THINK the women's libbers were all that active during the Occupation, but that has got to be a woman football player, right?

Prices for these are given as mint. Subtract twenty-five to fifty percent for damaged items. Yet even damaged celluloid items have some value.

*Top Row:*
| | |
|---|---|
| Dancers, Working Key Wind | $25.00-30.00 |
|   Non Working | 12.50-15.00 |
| Reindeer | 10.00-12.50 |
| Baby Rattle | 17.50-20.00 |

*2nd Row:*
| | |
|---|---|
| Baby Rattle | 17.50-20.00 |
| Dog | 10.00-12.50 |
| Doll, Movable Legs | 17.50-20.00 |

*3rd Row:*
| | |
|---|---|
| Pig (Tape Measure) | 17.50-20.00 |
| Doll (Bisque-Like) | 15.00-17.50 |
| Scottie Dog, Working Key Wind | 25.00-30.00 |
|   Non Working | 12.50-15.00 |

*Bottom:*
| | |
|---|---|
| Composition Doll | 17.50-20.00 |
| Negro Doll, Mint w/Clothes | 35.00-40.00 |
|   As Pictured | 15.00-20.00 |
| 12" Doll, Mint | 35.00-40.00 |
|   Some Damage | 15.00-20.00 |
| 5" Doll, Mint | 20.00-25.00 |
|   Some Damage, as shown | 10.00-12.50 |
| Football Player | 15.00-17.50 |

# CHILDREN'S TEA SETS

These sets were cheaply produced in quantity and many, today, will still be found in their original boxes. I assume dutiful mothers either wouldn't let their daughters play with glass dishes, or children back then were a lot more careful than MY two are!

These sets came in two, three, four, five and even six piece place settings. Some of the more elaborate ones featured meat platters and covered tureens. Naturally, having the original box will add two or three dollars to the value of the sets.

The blue-white set in the picture is commonly called the "Blue Wilow" set; none of the others seem to have names.

Place Settings:

| | |
|---|---|
| Two | $25.00-30.00 |
| Three | 35.00-40.00 |
| Four | 50.00-55.00 |
| Four w/Tureen and Platter | 65.00-70.00 |
| Five | 85.00-95.00 |
| Six | 125.00-150.00 |

*Blue Willow set will bring 50 percent more per set due to popularity and demand.

# CUP and SAUCER SETS

The colors, quality and decoration to be found in the cup and saucer sets are legion. You may find complete dinnerware sets in those marked "Cherry China"; however, most were solitary decorative pieces or small demitasse sets of four, six, or eight. The "Cherry China" sets shown here are found in the top row, middle and to its right; 3rd row, middle; and 4th row, second from the left.

Personally, were I to collect cups and saucers, I'd choose the smaller ones; I'm particularly charmed with the hexagonal cup and saucer at the upper right. Unfortunately, the cup is minus its handle; but its unusual shape got it photographed anyway.

I regret that the inside of some of the cups couldn't be seen since the interior is often more decorative than the outside—evidencing the Oriental thought of pleasing the eye while in the actual process of drinking.

The cup at top left was purchased from the estate of a gift shop which closed in 1953. All cups purchased from the estate had saucers except the twenty like this one. It leads one to speculate that it was never accompanied by a saucer.

*Top Row:*
    Cup (Saucer?)      $6.00- 6.50
    Demi/Set      10.00-12.50
    Cherry China Sets      8.00-12.00
    Hexagonal Demitasse Set      10.00-12.00
*2nd Row:*
    1st and 4th Sets      6.00- 7.50
    2nd and 5th Demitasse Sets      10.00-12.00
    Middle Set      12.50-15.00
*3rd Row:*
    1st and 2nd Sets      9.00-11.00
    3rd and 4th Sets      12.50-15.00
    5th Cup      12.50-15.00
*4th Row:*
    1st Demitasse Set      12.50-15.00
    2nd and 4th Sets      10.00-12.00
    Middle Set      15.00-20.00
    5th Demitasse Set      5.00- 6.00
*5th Row:*
    1st Set      10.00-12.00
    2nd and 4th Sets      10.00-12.50
    Middle Set      15.00-20.00
    5th Set, Souvenir Santa Claus, Ind.      12.50-15.00

# DECORATIVE ITEMS

All of the plates and plaques pictured here are wall decorations made with hangers, or places to which hangers attach, except for the two trays and the plate at the top. This plate is marked "Noritake—Made in Occupied Japan" and was part of a dinnerware set. You will notice that many of these are not as flamboyantly colorful as are the hanging wall decorations of today. Still and all, I'm certain that almost any "Occupied Japan" collector from Ohio would love to have the "map" of the "Buckeye" state. The placidity of the sailboat scene has appeal, also.

*Top Row:*
| | |
|---|---|
| Plate "Noritake" | $8.00-10.00 |

*2nd Row:*
| | |
|---|---|
| Hexagonal Plate | 3.00- 3.50 |
| 2nd and 4th Plates | 3.00- 3.50 |
| 3rd Plate | 7.00- 8.00 |
| 5th Plate | 2.00- 2.50 |

*3rd Row:*
| | |
|---|---|
| Plate, Souvenir of Oklahoma City, Okla. | 4.00- 5.00 |
| 2nd Plate w/Sailboat | 7.00- 7.50 |
| Ohio Map | 10.00-12.50 |
| Celery | 5.00- 6.00 |

*4th Row:*
| | |
|---|---|
| Violet Plate | 12.50-15.00 |
| Fruit Plate | 10.00-12.50 |
| Flower Plate | 10.00-12.50 |

*Bottom:*
| | |
|---|---|
| 1st Plate | 2.00- 2.50 |
| Bonbon Tray | 7.50- 8.50 |
| Flower Plate | 6.00- 7.50 |

# DINNERWARE

This set is "Cherry China"; it says just that and nothing else save the "Made in Occupied Japan." There, seemingly, were different patterns of "Cherry China" just as there were different patterns of "Noritake" made during the period of Occupation.

Shown here are four place settings of a set of twelve which includes dinner, salad, and bread and butter plates; dessert and soup bowls; cups and saucers; platter and serving pieces.

Cherry China,
    8 Place Setting w/Serving Pieces                 $175.00-250.00
    12 Place Setting w/Serving Pieces              250.00-350.00
Noritake China,
    8 Place Setting w/Serving Pieces                 200.00-250.00
    12 Place Setting w/Serving Pieces              250.00-450.00

# FISH BOWL ITEMS

All items, save the Evansville department store fish bowl recently acquired, are marked "Occupied Japan." The seated figures at the top and bottom are made for the top of the fish bowls, the boys supposedly holding fishing poles. I have never been fortunate enough to find any poles that survived the quarter century, but there must be a few.

The two cats menacing the edge both have gold fish in their mouths, evidence of their successful hanging in there; the brown one has now lost a leg, however, to my two year old's curiosity.

Mermaid and gold fish are now residing in their respective aquarium homes, the mermaid having entranced my Mom's fish since I was but a wee thing.

| | |
|---|---|
| *Top Row:* | |
| Ship | $9.00-10.00 |
| Bisque Boy and Girl | 17.50-22.50 |
| Castle | 6.00- 7.00 |
| Bisque Boy | 15.00-17.50 |
| *2nd Row:* | |
| Castle | 4.00- 5.00 |
| Cats | 17.50-20.00 |
| Goldfish | 8.00-10.00 |
| Bisque Boy and Girl | 12.50-15.00 |
| *Bottom:* | |
| Castle Atop Bridge | 8.00-10.00 |
| Pagoda Bridge | 10.00-12.00 |
| Mermaid | 17.50-20.00 |

# GLASS OBJECTS

There appears to be a meager amount of glass objects marked as being made in "Occupied Japan." Aside from the obvious reason of breakage, many of the glass objects carried only a sticker which said, "Made in Occupied Japan." Most of these were purposely removed, washed off or lost over the last twenty-five years.

The perfume bottles and cologne were probably parts of sets originally. I found the blue bottle and tray about five years ago at a garage sale and gave them to a friend who had a lot of "Occupied Japan." Needless to say, when time came for this book, I revisited her cache and borrowed these back along with a few of her other choice pieces, one of which is the Iris vase featured on the cover. All the bottles, tray and shakers have "Made in Occupied Japan" embossed on their bases.

The metal stand and metal bases of the glass shakers are marked as is the base of the ash tray sporting a real flower and butterfly under its glass dome.

The Myna sport glasses case, as well as the glasses themselves, are both marked. If you look closely, you can see the marking on the strap of the case.

|  |  |
|---|---|
| *Top Row:* | |
| Blue Cologne and Tray | $22.50-27.50/11.00-13.50 ea. |
| *2nd Row:* | |
| Perfume | 17.50 |
| w/atomizer | 30.00 |
| Duck, w/Sticker | 6.50-7.50 |
| Pink Cologne or Perfume | 17.50-20.00 |
| *3rd Row:* | |
| Shakers | 15.00-17.50 |
| Dogs, w/Sticker | 30.00-32.50 set |
| Shakers, w/Stand | 20.00-22.50 |
| *4th Row:* | |
| Sport Glasses | 25.00 |
| w/case | 35.00 |
| Ash Tray | 15.00-20.00 |

# LAMPS

Occupied Japanese lamps usually come in pairs, are most often small boudoir lamps and, more than likely, will have a couple whose position will be reversed on the opposite lamp. The colonial pair at bottom left are typical of this type lamp.

Now, the Lacquerware lamp, shown again, blows all the generalities just given above. It is large, probably a living room lamp, has no figures on it and probably was a solitary lamp instead of a pair.

All of these lamps have cords and work, save the one lacking the socket, of course.

| | |
|---|---|
| Lacquerware Lamp | $35.00-40.00 |
| Colonial Single | 27.50-30.00 |
| Colonial Single, sans Socket | 25.00-30.00 |
| w/socket | 35.00-40.00 |
| Colonial Pair, Left | 50.00-60.00 |
| Pair Lamps, Right | 50.00-60.00 |

# LACQUERWARE

For those of you not familiar with lacquerware, it is a wood, or sometime metal, based object coated with a highly polished coat of lacquer common to China and Japan. All items here, save for the dancers placed on the shelves of the stand at the bottom, are of lacquerware.

The inside of the ice bucket and the tongs are silver-plated; and the lamp socket is plastic. You may notice that the finish for the white tree on the lamp base has rubbed off; it seems not to have been coated with lacquer as was the rest of the lamp.

Lacquered items are difficult to find; so be on the lookout for them. Most will be stamped in gold markings, particularly black objects.

| | |
|---|---|
| Plates | $4.50- 5.00 |
| Coasters, 2 Sizes | 2.50- 3.00 |
| Wall Shelf Unit | 35.00-40.00 |
| Lamp Base | 35.00-40.00 |
| Ice Bucket and Tongs | 30.00-35.00 |
| Salad Bowl w/Fork and Spoon | 27.50-30.00 |
| Bowl w/6 Individual Bowls and Spoon | 25.00-30.00 |

# LIGHTERS and MISCELLANEOUS METAL OBJECTS

Novelty items, such as lighters, must have given some Japanese sleepless nights just trying to think up objects to stick a lighter in! The strangest location for one here is in the eraser end of the mechanical pencil at the lower edge of the photograph. The pencil end actually writes; so you either weren't to make any mistakes—or you were to burn them. We put a little lighter fluid in it at the photography session to check for spoofing, but it really works!

The donkey jewel chest is neat; but so is my dime bulldog pencil sharpener. I found him at a garage sale and didn't find the bonus "Occupied Japan" under the blades until later when I was cleaning it.

You can tell how cheap the altimony metal is by looking at the dime store trophies that show that telltale corrosion that still shines through after cleaning.

| | |
|---|---|
| *Top Row:* | |
| Lamp Lighter | $15.00-17.50 |
| Donkey Lighter | 20.00-22.50 |
| Boot Lighter | 7.50-8.50 |
| *2nd Row:* | |
| Coat of Armor Lighter | 15.00-17.50 |
| Inlaid Lighter | 12.50-15.00 |
| Mint Compote | 5.00-6.00 |
| Table Gun Lighter | 20.00-22.50 |
| Shoe Pin Cushion | 7.50-8.00 |
| *3rd Row:* | |
| Table Lighter | 5.00- 6.00 |
| Gun Lighter | 12.00-13.50 |
| Bulldog Pencil Sharpener | 8.00- 9.50 |
| Shaker and Mustard Set w/Tray | 20.00-22.50 |
| Trophies | 2.00- 2.50 |
| Donkey Jewel Chest | 15.00-17.50 |
| *Bottom:* | |
| Tea Holder | 12.00-15.00 |
| Nut Dish | 5.00-6.00 |
| Key Lighter | 7.50-10.00 |
| Pencil Lighter | 15.00-20.00 |

# NOVELTY ITEMS

Except for souvenir items which were priced higher, you will find that these were dime store items ranging in price from 10¢—29¢ originally; at least, that's about the highest price I can find stamped on any of these. Dual pieces, like Martha and George here, went all the way up to 59¢! The souvenir Lookout Mountain pitcher was stamped 39¢. Many times you can buy these little trinkets very reasonably since people don't check to see if they have any markings or they just haven't caught up with the fact that "Occupied Japan" is beginning to weave a special magic.

The little trays with the tiny pieces on them at the bottom are quite rare complete, as these pieces were easily misplaced.

*Top Row:*
    All Items Save 2nd Teapot      $3.50- 4.00
    2nd Teapot w/Removable Lid      5.00- 6.00
*2nd Row:*
    All Items Save Half Potty and Lookout Mt. Pitcher      3.50- 4.00
    Half Potty      3.00- 3.50
    Lookout Mt. Pitcher      3.00- 3.50
*3rd Row:*
    All Items Save Martha/George and Floral Vase      2.50- 3.00
    Martha and George Set      12.50- 15.00
    Blue Floral Vase      7.00- 7.50
*4th Row:*
    All Items      3.50- 4.00
*5th Row:*
    All Items Save Small Trays and Nude Boy      3.50- 4.00
    Nude Boy      4.50- 5.00
    Tray w/6 Pieces
      Removable Lid on Pitcher      17.50 (complete)
      Incomplete      2.00 each piece
    Only the trays are marked "Made in Occupied Japan."

# PAPER and WOOD PRODUCTS

This is by far the most fascinating page in the book as far as a collector is concerned. Some of these items are practically unbelievable. Consider the three little umbrellas which have never been opened or would have lost their paper bands identifying them as "Occupied Japan" objects. Too, the "Rag Time Band" of extremely thin plastic is probably still intact only due to the box. Each member plays a different, delicate instrument from clarinet to bass fiddle.

The sun-faded Santa and the Christmas star have tags identifying their place of origin.

The doll's chest of drawers not only has three working drawers and a mirrored door; but the work on the exterior is inlay and must have taken forever!

The wooden box on the bottom row has a sliding panel (well camouflaged, I can testify) which reveals a notch which, when pressed, opens a secret drawer compartment (shown opened). I've seen similar boxes, even some with the same design, but this is the first I've run into with the magic words marking it.

I left the little black box until last, creme de la creme, so to speak. This is the 1950 version of our modern day Polaroid. Yes, this little box took and developed pictures—so it says. There's film in the camera and it did cross my mind to try it out; but, after discussing film longevity with myself, I didn't. It certainly is an unusual piece, however.

| | |
|---|---|
| Large Umbrella, approximately 3 ft. across | $25.00-30.00 |
| Wood Jewelry Box | 12.50-15.00 |
| Camera, Self Developing Film | 75.00-100.00 |
| Decorative Fan | 6.00- 7.00 |
| Small Umbrellas | 2.00- 3.00 |
| Christmas Ornament | 12.50-15.00 |
| Doll Chest | 25.00-30.00 |
| Box, Secret Opening | 25.00-30.00 |
| Ship (String and Wood) | 10.00-12.00 |
| Santa on Sleigh | 35.00-40.00 |
| Rag Time Band, Boxed Set (4.00 ea.) | 25.00-30.00 |

# PLANTERS (Primarily Animal)

Had the boat been a little older vintage, I might have gotten by with calling it Noah's Ark and saved that long word in the heading.

Most of the planters are made very cheaply out of a soft, porous material. The little donkey on the bottom row left is the only planter here of much quality of workmanship. Since these were generally of the 19¢—59¢ variety, it should surprise us only that the design and workmanship is as good as it is. These HAVE lasted a quarter century, too, so that should say something positive about them.

*Top Row:*
    All Items Save Bee          $5.00- 6.00
    Bee          6.50- 7.50
*2nd Row:*
    All Items Save Rabbit          5.50- 7.00
    Rabbit          7.50- 9.00
*3rd Row:*
    All Items          5.00- 6.50
*4th Row:*
    Duck and Donkey          5.50- 6.50
    Boat          15.00-17.50
*5th Row:*
    Donkey, Left          10.00-12.00
    Donkey, Center          8.00-10.00
    Zebra          8.00-10.00

# PLANTERS—People

Just as with the animal planters, quality materials weren't generally used. Yet, some of the workmanship is surprisingly detailed. The exceptions to this general pattern here involve the oriental heads on the top row. These are made from good grade porcelain.

Quality material and workmanship always add to the desirability of anything collected, and that is no less true for "Occupied Japan" collectors when there is quality to be had.

| | |
|---|---|
| *Top Row:* | |
| Small Girl | $3.50- 4.00 |
| Oriental Heads | 22.50-25.00 |
| *2nd Row:* | |
| 1st and 4th Planters | 7.50-10.00 |
| 2nd and 3rd Planters/bookends | 12.50-15.00 |
| *3rd Row:* | |
| All Items | 7.50-10.00 |
| *4th Row:* | |
| All Items Save Center Pieces | 8.00-10.00 |
| Tall Center Pieces | 12.50-15.00 |

# SALT and PEPPER SHAKERS

Needless to say, it was great to have a salt and pepper shaker collector in the family when time came for this page—even if my Mom didn't have the faintest idea whether or not any of those innumerable sets she had gained over the years were "Occupied Japan!" You're seeing a lot of what were.

I want you to remember, too, that the prices listed here are meant as a guide. You have to be the final judge of how much you are willing to pay for something you want. As with anything else, you can find shakers of good quality materials and workmanship and then, others... Also, items such as salt and pepper shakers bring higher prices due to people (like my Mom) who collect shakers regardless of markings.

Three piece sets, where the shakers rest on a base of some sort, are usually marked on the basepiece only. The bottom of the shakers will say "Japan" if they are marked at all.

*Top Row:*
    All Items Save Windmills and Toby Shakers      $10.00-12.00 pr.
    Windmills & Toby      12.50-15.00 pr.
*2nd Row:*
    All Items Save Martha and George      10.00-12.00 pr.
    Martha and George      15.00-20.00 pr.
*3rd Row:*
    All Items Save Frogs      10.00-12.00 pr.
    Frogs      15.00-20.00 pr.
*4th Row:*
    Three Piece Sets      17.50-20.00
*5th Row:*
    Three Piece Sets, Save Cucumbers      17.50-20.00
    Cucumbers      20.00-25.00

# SALT and PEPPER SHAKERS

Here are some of the more expensive types of shakers due to materials used, collectibility, or both. You will notice four lonesome singles for whom no mates turned up. You see some that were also pictured in other categories, such as glass or metal.

*Top Row:*

| | |
|---|---|
| Chicken and Girl | $6.00- 7.50 ea. |
| Boats/3 Piece Sets | 15.00-17.50 |
| Gaily Decorated | 17.50-20.00 |

*2nd Row:*

| | |
|---|---|
| 4 Piece Metal Set | 20.00-22.50 |
| Glass Shakers and Metal Stand | 20.00-22.50 |
| Hobnail Shakers | 15.00-17.50 pr. |
| Frogs/3 Piece Set | 15.00-20.00 |
| Clown | 8.00-10.00 |

*3rd Row:*

| | |
|---|---|
| Tomato, Pr. | 6.00- 8.00 |
| Tomato Sets on Leaf w/Mustard | 15.00-20.00 |

*4th Row:*

| | |
|---|---|
| Blue/White Shakers | |
| (Match egg cup pictured on page 17) | 15.00-20.00 pr. |
| Windmills w/Moving Blades | 25.00-30.00 pr. |
| Negro Cooks, Pr. | 35.00-40.00 pr. |
| Cottages and Peppers | 8.00-10.00 |
| Boy | 6.00- 7.50 |

*5th Row:*

| | |
|---|---|
| Beehive Set | 20.00-25.00 |
| Beehive Sugar and Marmalade | 20.00-22.50 |
| Separate Sugar | 10.00-12.50 |
| Ceramic Set on Tray | 20.00-25.00 |

# SOUVENIR ITEMS

By far, the biggest single market for "Occupied Japan" items was the souvenir trade. You could get items already imprinted or you could attach a sticker to them from anywhere in the U.S.A. or Canada.

The spinning cable car from San Francisco might be the most interesting item to a Californian, the Ohio "map" might please someone from Cincinnati, or the race horse ash tray might most attract a Kentuckian, like myself. What I'm saying is that prices on souvenir items are speculative. The Lexington, Ky. souvenir ash tray with galloping horses might not be worth as much to someone in Michigan as it would to someone from or in Kentucky. Then, again, someone who loves "horsey" items, or who collects George and Martha, or who has a passion for cats might just be delighted to get such a piece for his collection.

| | |
|---|---|
| *Top Row:* | |
| Statue, Flat Gap, Ky. | $15.00-17.50 |
| Pitcher, Lookout Mt., Tenn. | 3.50- 4.00 |
| Statue, Canadian National Exhibition | 12.00-14.00 |
| *2nd Row:* | |
| Toothpick, Wisconsin | 5.00- 5.50 |
| Cats, Niagara Falls, Canada | 8.00-10.00 |
| Plate, Oklahoma City, Okla. | 3.25- 4.00 |
| Vase, Canada | 5.00- 6.00 |
| Cup and Saucer, Santa Claus, Ind. | 12.50-15.00 |
| Pitchers, Mt. Vernon, Va., pr. | 12.50-15.00 |
| *3rd Row:* | |
| Tray, New York City | 2.50- 3.00 |
| Tray, St. Louis Zoo | 2.50- 3.00 |
| Tray, Catskill Mts. | 2.50- 3.00 |
| *4th Row:* | |
| Ash Tray, Lexington, Ky. | 5.00- 6.00 |
| Map Dish, Ohio or Other States | 10.00-12.50 |
| Ash Tray, San Francisco | 20.00-22.50 |

# TEA SETS

Lovely, complete tea sets can be found. More than likely, however, you will run into the innumerable partial sets. So consider yourself lucky if you find a complete one. Yet, don't pass by a partial set that you really like if it's got the essential pieces. It's possible that the remaining pieces will turn up in some shop or garage sale; in fact, I've had several first hand accounts of just such happenings.

Prices here and on the next page will reflect only what is shown. You will have to use your own judgment on complete sets.

The set in the second row is complete except for the plate on which the shakers and mustard sit.

|  |  |
|---|---|
| *Top Row:* | |
| Sugar, Left | $15.00-17.50 |
| Teapot, Sugar and Creamer | 50.00-75.00 |
| Individual Teapot | 15.00-17.50 |
| *2nd Row:* | |
| As Shown | 90.00-100.00 |
| *3rd Row:* | |
| Creamer and Sugar | 15.00-17.50 |
| Teapot | 17.50-20.00 |

55

# TEA SETS

I regret you can't see the true beauty of the square bowl because of the dulling mist sprayed on by the photographer. This fine piece of china reflected the light so brightly that the picture could not be taken until it was "toned down." This bowl rings as good china does. The other items photographed "true" to their natural colorings.

The handle of the candy dish is made of flexible bamboo and can be removed or attached in other places.

*Top Row:*
    Tea Set                                            $60.00-75.00
*Middle:*
    Bowl                                              20.00–25.00
    Square Flat Dish                         12.50-15.00
*Bottom:*
    Cup and Saucer Set w/Stand           45.00-55.00
    Candy Dish                                 15.00-17.50

# TOBY MUGS, ETC.

Toby mugs are collected world wide; these are cheap imitations of the English ones but were quite popular.

The fourth row consists of only head figurines; but they seemed to fit well here, so they were included by the photographer.

The mug on the bottom row, right, is of the Supreme Allied Commander of the Occupational Zone, General Douglas MacArthur.

The barrel mug next to MacArthur is not a Toby since the handle is a person and the mug is a barrel. This type mug is, however, highly collectible; so watch for them. I sold five different mugs of this type a few years ago; so there's bound to be a whole set of them. You may run into a risque one or two having nude ladies for handles. That will give you guys a chance to "have your cup and drink it, too."

*Top Row:*
    All Toby Mugs                                           $15.00-17.50
*2nd Row:*
    All Toby Mugs Save 3rd from Left      15.00-20.00
    3rd Roby Mug from Left             20.00-25.00
*3rd Row:*
    Tobies, Either End                 25.00-27.50
    Other Toby Mugs                 15.00-17.50
*4th Row:*
    Large Heads                       22.50-25.00
    Small Heads                     12.00-15.00
*5th Row:*
    1st Two Toby Mugs                12.50-15.00
    3rd Toby                          25.00-30.00
    Barrel Mug                      15.00-20.00
    MacArthur Toby                50.00-65.00

# TOOTHPICKS and BUD VASES

You may grab your toothpick from a clown, painter, baby carriage, wagon—even a topless lady. Bud vases, likewise, come adorned by various personages; angels, naked girls, honest workers, femme fatales. The Japanese certainly didn't discriminate.

Since my wife will edit this, I guess I'll choose the angel on the shooting star in row four as my favorite; there's one on the row above that did catch my fancy.

| | |
|---|---|
| *Top Row:* | |
| All Items | $4.00- 5.00 |
| *2nd Row:* | |
| All Items Save Liberated Girl | 4.00- 5.00 |
| Topless Girl | 8.00-10.00 |
| *3rd Row:* | |
| All Items, Save Naked Girl and Wagon | 3.00- 3.50 |
| Naked Girl and Vase | 8.00-10.00 |
| Girl w/Wagon | 10.00-12.00 |
| *4th Row:* | |
| All Items, Save Angel on Star | 4.50- 6.50 |
| Angel on Shooting Star | 8.00-10.00 |
| *5th Row:* | |
| All Items, Save Tree | 7.00- 8.00 |
| Tree | 4.50- 5.00 |

# TOYS

The stories of how some of these survived through the years would make a book in itself! All of these items work except the bug. Somebody seems to have tried to squash him in his hindermost section. The elephant and bear dance, the squirrel hops and the mouse circles.

I find myself wondering what sort of person wore the stick pin fly—or how many unsuspecting housewives tried to "kill" one to somebody's glee.

The box of puzzles is the most exciting thing here. If you look closely at the sheriff's badge in the front row, you can read the "Occupied Japan" on it. This set of fifteen puzzles has the original top and instructions on how to work the puzzles. As a mathematician, I enjoy puzzles; but a couple of these are really tough! (Editor's note: collecting and writing is all such WORK, you know.)

*Top Row:*
    Dancing Elephant in Original Box                    $30.00-35.00
    Dancing Bear in Original Box                       25.00-30.00
    Hopping Squirrel                                    25.00-30.00
*2nd Row:*
    Running Mouse in Original Box                   17.50-20.00
    Wind Up Car                                    12.50-15.00
    Baby Jeep in Box                               12.50-15.00
*3rd Row:*
    Car w/Box                                      12.50-15.00
    Fly Pin on Card                               4.50- 5.00
    Beetle                                          17.50-20.00
    Watches on Card                          10.00-12.50 ea.
*Bottom:*
    Box of Puzzles w/Instructions                 50.00-65.00

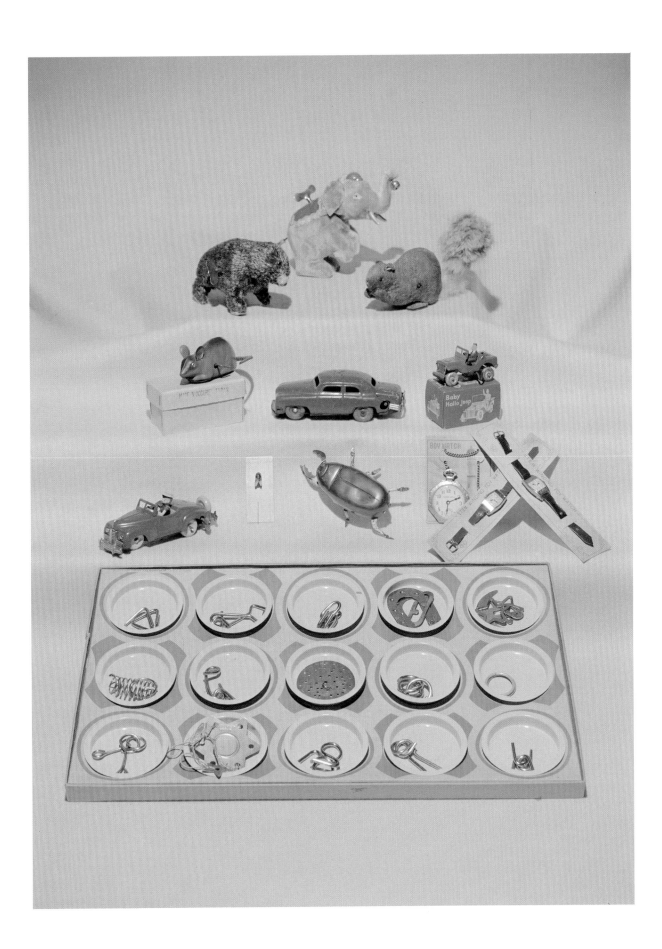

# VASES—Small

These tiny vases were made mostly for decorating, but they would serve as bud vases if desired. The various orange, brown and blue vases with oriental figures throughout the picture are known as Kutani–ware.

As you can tell from the picture, many of these came in pairs and some collectors will buy them only that way. I'm not that exacting; and, besides, no matter how small, two vases take up more room than one.

*Top Row: (Left to Right)*
| | |
|---|---|
| All Vases, Save 5th and 6th | $4.00- 6.00 ea. |
| 5th Vase, Looks Like Egyptian Hieroglyphics | 8.00-10.00 |
| 6th, Kutani-Type | 3.00- 4.50 |

*2nd Row:*
| | |
|---|---|
| All Save 4th Pair | 5.00- 6.50 |
| 4th Pair, Kutani-type | 8.00- 9.50 pr. |

*3rd Row:*
| | |
|---|---|
| Six Kutani-types | 5.00- 6.50 |
| 2nd Vase (unusual shape) | 6.00- 7.50 |
| 6th, 7th, 8th Vases | 3.00- 4.50 ea. |

*4th Row:*
| | |
|---|---|
| Six Kutani-Types | 5.00- 6.00 ea. |
| Others | 3.00- 3.50 ea. |

*Bottom:*
| | |
|---|---|
| All Vases | 3.00- 4.50 ea. |

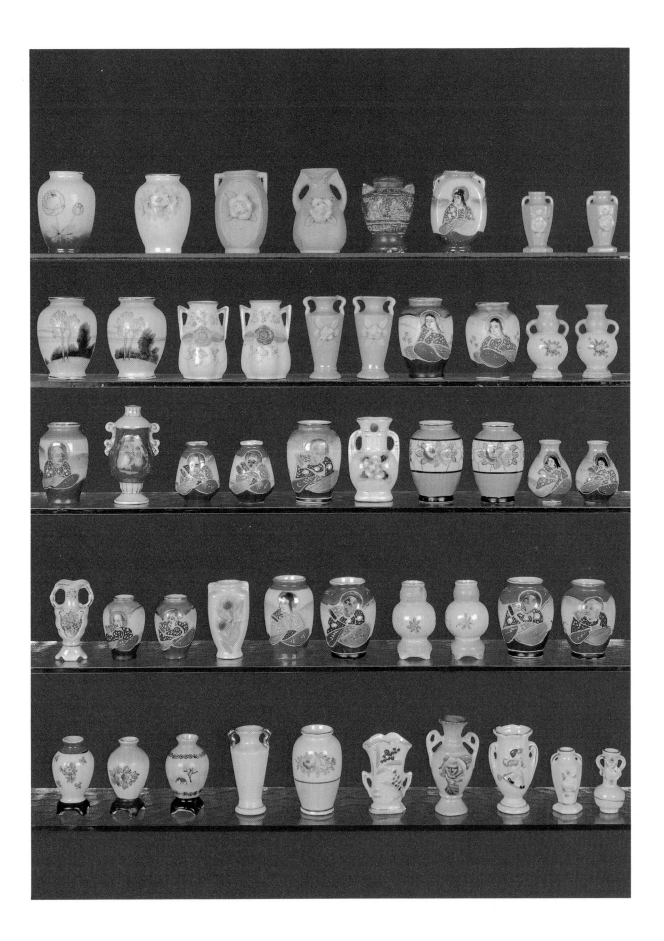

# VASES—Large

The vases on the bottom shelf mostly represent better quality "Occupied Japan" vases. The others are pretty much the common, everyday variety. I tried to buy the two larger vases from my friend who had the cache of "Occupied Japan" goodies; but she happens to be a member of the Lexington Iris Society, so you can imagine just how far I got there.

I'm partial to the two vases with the little Japanese figures seated on, or in, them. These are rather unusual, and should lend interest in even the most discriminating of settings.

*Top Row:*
    All Vases          $4.50- 7.00 ea.
*2nd Row:*
    All Vases Save 2nd and 5th      6.50- 7.50 ea.
    2nd Vase, Children      8.00- 9.50
    5th Vase, Seated Figure      20.00-22.50
*3rd Row:*
    All Vases Save George Washington      5.00- 6.00
    George Washington      7.50- 9.00
*Bottom:*
    1st Vase, Fine Quality      20.00-25.00
    Iris Vases      30.00-35.00 ea.
    4th Vase, Enclosed Figure      25.00-30.00
    5th Vase      10.00-12.50

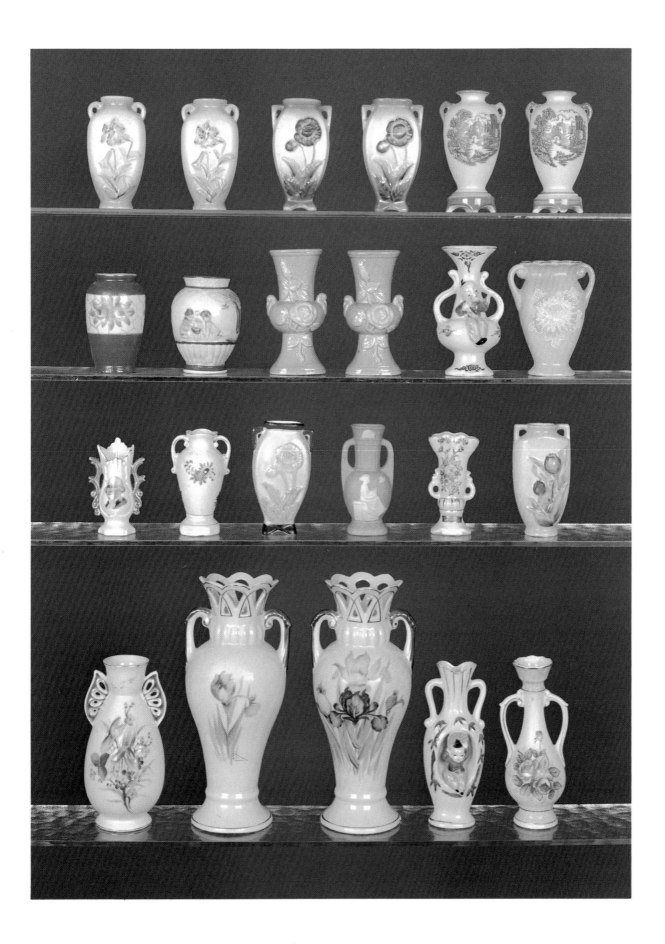

# FIGURINES

## ANGELS and ELVES

These are certainly among the most adorable of the figurine characters. The small angel watching over the sleeping child is Hummel-like in appearance while the impish faces of the elves with the planter backs contrast with this angelic scene.

There's an entire set of elves riding insects such as butterflies and dragonflies; but all I could find when I started looking were the two praying mantis riders.

*Top Row:*
|  |  |
|---|---|
| Elf on Praying Mantis | $20.00-25.00 |
| Angel | 4.00- 5.00 |

*Middle:*
|  |  |
|---|---|
| Seated Elves with Planters | 15.00-20.00 |
| Angel w/Flute | 7.50- 9.00 |

*Bottom:*
|  |  |
|---|---|
| Seated Elf | 12.50-15.00 |
| Reclining Elf | 12.50-15.00 |
| Angel w/Sleeping Child | 25.00-30.00 |
| Standing Angel | 6.00- 8.00 |

# BISQUE FIGURINES

From the tiny seated boy to the large standing lady, the quality of workmanship in these figurines is comparable to the work that is found today in the better gift shops at prices twice those of "Occupied Japan" figurines which are twenty-five years old. To me, it seems foolish to buy something new when, for less money, you can buy something old and have a collectible besides. Of course, the new is readily available and the older, collectible piece may take a little more looking.

*Top Row:*

| | |
|---|---|
| Peasant Girl Standing | $20.00-25.00 |
| Farmer w/Rake | 20.00-25.00 |
| M'Lady w/Dove | 60.00-75.00 |
| Peasant Boy | 20.00-25.00 |
| Seated Girl | 22.50-25.00 |

*Middle:*

| | |
|---|---|
| Man w/Cane | 17.50-20.00 |
| Boy w/Dog | 20.00-25.00 |

*Bottom:*

| | |
|---|---|
| Boy Holding Mug | 17.50-20.00 |
| Standing Lady w/Hat | 17.50-20.00 |
| Lad w/Cloak | 17.50-20.00 |
| Seated Little Boy | 15.00-17.50 |
| Standing Dowager | 15.00-17.50 |
| Peasant Lass | 10.00-12.50 |
| M'Lord Standing | 25.00-30.00 |

# BISQUE PAIRS and SHELF SITTERS

Somehow the pastel colors of bisque pairs add immeasurable beauty to a mantle or book shelf. The bisque plaques will do the same in a special place on a wall; and, as stated previously, why buy new figurines when the older ones aren't that hard to find and are collectible also?

The shelf sitters are in a class to themselves. Naturally, the biggest difficulty here is bumping them once—usually once is the only chance you get. Needless to say, in an earthquake zone, I wouldn't collect these. They do help make ordinary shelves into something unique.

*Top Row:*
    Boy and Girl Pair          $60.00-80.00
*2nd Row:*
    Seated Musician Pair          45.00-60.00
    Plaques Pair, Mint          45.00-50.00
    Boys Holding Leaves          35.00-40.00 ea.
*3rd and 4th Row:*
    Girl and Boy on Left, Pr.          37.50-45.00
    Seated Boy and Girl          17.50-22.50
    Japanese Pair          25.00-30.00
    Man and Woman on Right, Pr.          40.00-50.00
*Bottom:*
    All Seated Figures          15.00-17.50

# CHILDREN

The following three pictures show the realm of children. Some of these are quality items while others are not. Many occur in pairs.

*Top Row:*
    All Items Save Center Boy w/duck      $6.00- 7.50
    Boy w/Duck      10.00-12.50
*2nd Row:*
    All Items Save Reclining girl      5.00- 6.00
    Reclining Girl w/Bird      8.00-10.00
*3rd Row:*
    All Items      4.00- 5.00
*4th Row:*
    1st Five Items      5.00- 6.00
    Last Five Items      10.00-15.00
*5th Row:*
    Boy and Dog, Left      17.50-20.00
    Remaining Items      12.50-17.50

# CHILDREN MUSICIANS

From drum to violin, the musical gamut is run. All instruments may not be shown here, but I'd bet you could find almost any kind if you looked a bit.

*Top Row:*

    All Items Save Clarinet Player and Drummer     $5.00- 6.00

    Clarinet Player and Bisque Drummer     10.00-15.00

*Middle:*

    All Items Save Small Figure in Front     8.00-10.00

    Small Figure (Gabriel?)     4.00- 5.50

*Bottom:*

    All Items Save Last     5.00- 7.00

    Last Boy and Dog     12.50-15.00

# CHILDREN: Shelf Sitters, et al.

Obviously the easiest broken of all figurines but, by far the most interesting, are the shelf sitters—be they crossed leg, straight leg, leg under knee or crooked knee!

The little girl at the top with the picnic basket has even taken along a bottle of wine. Frankly, she looks a little young for the "book and thou" bit; so maybe the water's just bad.

*Top Row:*
    Shelf Sitters      $15.00-17.50
    Boy and Girl at Ends      5.00-6.00
    Middle Two Girls      15.00-17.50
*Middle:*
    Shelf Sitters      15.00-17.50
    Boy and Girl in Center      4.00- 6.00
    Girl in White      3.00- 4.00
*Bottom:*
    Shelf Sitters      15.00-17.50
    Tall Girl w/Doll      8.00-10.00
    Small girl w/Doll      8.00-10.00

# DANCING GIRLS

If you can remember the 1930's and early 1940's, you should recognize the styles of dress for most of these dancers. The lady in the center looks more like she's fighting the wind than dancing, though.

*Top Row:*
    Ballerina      $30.00-35.00
    White Dress Dancer      15.00-17.50
    Pink Dress Dancer      10.00-12.50
    Lavender Dress Dancer      15.00-20.00
*Middle:*
    Girl Ballerina and Green Dress Dancer      10.00-12.00
    Tall Girl w/Hat      25.00-30.00
*Bottom:*
    All Dancers      9.00-10.00

# DANCING PAIRS

Two of these dancing couples are just one statue while the others are matching pairs.

It is frustrating to try to match pairs because their bases and markings have to be the same; many times they will be quite similar, but not matching. So be forewarned should you try to find a mate for your single dancer.

The most popular style of dancers are the Colonial-dressed pairs with men in their wigs and women in their bouffant dresses.

*Top Row:*
    Boy and Girl                     $12.50-15.00
*2nd Row:*
    Colonial Man and Woman, Pr.     20.00-22.50
    Pr. Middle Left               10.00-12.00
    Center Pair                  9.00-10.00
    Pr., Middle Right          12.00-14.00
    Colonial Man and Woman      20.00-22.50
*Bottom:*
    Taller Couple              25.00-27.50
    Center Pair                12.50-15.00
    Couple at Right           17.50-20.00

# DELFT BLUE FIGURINES

These figurines are among the more difficult pieces to obtain of all the "Occupied Japan" items. I'm irritated because I had purchased two other pieces to be photographed here; and, in packing all this host of material, I left them behind. As fill-in, we used again the blue-white windmills. Sorry.

In case you are not familiar with Delft, it is a blue-white china common to Holland which will explain the windmills. The two pieces which missed out were a Dutch boy and girl.

Evidently the painters of these statues thought the blue-white a little dull, so you can see the pink additions in three of the pieces. Personally, I think it adds to them; but, then, that's a matter of individual taste.

*Top Row:*
    Lady Holding Hat                                   $20.00-25.00
    Dutch Sailor w/Bag                               17.50-20.00
*Middle:*
    Lady w/Feathered Hat                          20.00-25.00
    Lady Holding Hat                                   20.00-25.00
*Bottom:*
    M'Lady w/Basket                                   25.00-30.00
    Dutch Girl                                         20.00-25.00
    Windmill Shakers                                12.50-15.00
    Windmill Shakers w/Turning Blades          25.00-30.00

84

# FIGURINES COUPLES and GROUPS

Several of these statues could pass for good European china if they were not marked "Occupied Japan." If you examine these closely, you will see how some statues are basically the same, just painted differently. Some figurines are alike save in size, also.

The bride and groom figurines are supposed to be among the rarer items, yet I'll bet there are a number of these around; they're just packed away in the attic as a keepsake along with the pressed bridal flowers and the wedding gown. I've seen yet another pair since photographing these two.

The man pushing the lady on the sleigh at the bottom of the picture is a fine piece as is the couple seated with the basket between their feet. You might also look for the groups of three as seen in the top row. These are not so plentiful.

*Top Row: (Left to Right)*
| | |
|---|---|
| 1st, 2nd, 4th and 7th Couple | $12.50-15.00 |
| 3rd Couple | 5.00-6.00 |
| 5th Couple | 4.50- 5.00 |
| 6th Group | 17.50-20.00 |

*2nd Row:*
| | |
|---|---|
| 1st, 2nd and 7th Couple | 12.50-15.00 |
| 3rd, 5th and 6th Couple | 5.50- 6.50 |
| 4th, Bride and Groom | 22.50-25.00 |

*3rd Row:*
| | |
|---|---|
| All Couples Save 6th | 12.50-15.00 |
| 6th couple | 5.50- 6.00 |

*4th Row:*
| | |
|---|---|
| 1st Couple, Fine Detail | 22.50-25.00 |
| 2nd and 5th Couples | 12.50-15.00 |
| 6th Couple, Canadian National Exposition Souvenir | 12.00-14.00 |
| 3rd Couple | 10.00-12.00 |
| Bride and Groom | 30.00-35.00 |
| 7th Couple | 15.00-17.50 |

*5th Row:*
| | |
|---|---|
| Man Pushing Sleigh | 45.00-50.00 |
| 2nd Couple | 25.00-30.00 |
| 3rd Couple | 30.00-35.00 |
| 4th Couple | 15.00-17.50 |

# MUSICIANS

Featured here are several tough to find pieces, as well as some figurines of quality workmanship. As mentioned previously, the groups with three people are hard to find; so watch for these in your travels. The piano ensemble on the third row is an example.

I'm not quite sure how many people would consider the organ grinder a musician; since the instrument is capable of rendering a tune, we included it. Besides, the little monkeys may consider them quite gifted.

The two bisque players in the fourth row lend quite an air of dignity to the organ grinders and fiddle player, don't they?

*Top Row:*

| | |
|---|---|
| 1st, 2nd and 5th Musicians | $5.50- 6.50 ea. |
| 3rd Figure | 12.50-15.00 |
| 4th Figure | 7.00- 8.00 |

*2nd Row:*

| | |
|---|---|
| 1st Figure | 5.00-6.00 |
| 2nd Figure | 3.00- 3.50 |
| 3rd Pair | 8.00-10.00 |
| 4th Figure | 3.50- 4.00 |
| 5th Figure | 8.00-10.00 |

*3rd Row:*

| | |
|---|---|
| 1st and 2nd Figures | 5.00- 6.00 |
| Girl and Piano | 15.00-17.50 |
| Piano Ensemble | 30.00-35.00 |
| Man and Piano | 17.50-20.00 |

*4th Row:*

| | |
|---|---|
| Seated Bisque Pair | 45.00-60.00 |
| Organ Grinders | 15.00-17.50 |
| 4th Man w/Fiddle | 12.50-15.00 |
| 6th and 7th Foursome | 25.00-30.00 pr. |

*5th Row:*

| | |
|---|---|
| Maid w/Suitor | 20.00-22.50 pr. |
| 3rd and 4th, Men | 12.50-15.00 |
| Seated Flutist | 12.50-15.00 |
| End Pair Musicians | 20.00-25.00 |

# ORIENTALS

You would expect a foreign country to turn out figurines in their own images as well as those of the country to where they're shipping; and the Japanese did not disappoint. They made numerous replicas of themselves from tiny shelf sitters to large figurines.

*Top Row:*
    Figures 1,3,5, and 6      $7.00- 9.00
    Bisque Figures 2 and 8      10.00-12.00
    Reclining Figure      10.00-12.00
    Small girl #7      6.00- 6.50

*2nd Row:*
    Figures 1 and 4      6.00- 7.50
    Rickshaw      17.50-20.00
    Man w/Clay Pots      9.00-11.00
    Shelf Sitter      15.00-17.50

*3rd Row:*
    Shelf Sitters      15.00-17.50
    Figures 2,3,4,5, and 9      6.00- 7.50
    Figure 6      4.00-5.00
    Bisque Girl #7      12.50-15.00

*4th Row:*
    Girls 1 and 7, Fine Detail      20.00-22.50
    Figures 2,5, and 6      15.00-20.00
    3rd Figures      15.00-20.00
    Tall Figure #4      30.00-40.00

# ORIENTAL PAIRS

Most of the figures here occur in male and female pairs; but there are some exceptions.

On the top row are two incense burners. Since these have come back in style, the demand for the more decorative ones has increased in recent years; thus the price increase.

Notice again the same figures with different colorings at each end of the lower shelf.

*Top Row:*
    Shelf Sitter                                   $15.00-17.50
    Figures 2 and 3                             5.50- 6.50 ea.
    Figures 4,7 and 8                         4.50- 6.00
    Incense burners                        14.00-16.00 ea.
*2nd Row:*
    Figures 1,2,3                              8.00-10.00
    Figures 4 and 5, Pr.                   17.50-20.00
    Figures 6 and 7                        6.00-7.00
*3rd Row:*
    Rickshaw                                17.50-20.00
    Bookends                              20.00-25.00 pr.
    Figures 4 and 5, pr.                   7.00-8.00
*Bottom:*
    Pair, Each End                           25.00-30.00
    Figures 3 and 4, ea.                   12.50-15.00
    Figures 5 and 6, pr.                   45.00-50.00

# PAIRS OF FIGURINES

As I have ventured to say several times before, matching pairs of figurines is a difficult task; and, with the exception of the first pair on the third row, all of these are paired as to base types and base markings. Most of these were bought as pairs, but I got lucky a few times in being able to match up pairs.

*Top Row:*

| | |
|---|---|
| 1st Pair | $3.50- 4.00 |
| Pairs 2 and 5 | 7.50-9.50 |
| 3rd Pair | 12.00-14.00 |
| 4th Pair | 25.00-30.00 |
| 6th Pair | 7.50-8.00 |

*2nd Row:*

| | |
|---|---|
| Pairs 1 and 5 | 15.00-17.50 |
| Pairs 2 and 3 | 10.00-12.00 |
| 4th Pair | 12.50-15.00 |

*3rd Row:*

| | |
|---|---|
| 1st and 2nd Figurines | 10.00-12.00 |
| Pairs 3 and 4 | 20.00-25.00 pr. |
| Pairs 5 and 6 | 10.00-12.50 pr. |

*4th Row:*

| | |
|---|---|
| Pairs 1 and 3, Nice Detail | 45.00-55.00 pr. |
| 2nd Pair, Signed Andrea | 60.00-75.00 pr. |

# SETS and PARTIAL SETS

The task involved with sets, of course, is to complete them. It's a chore to match up pairs, but not nearly so difficult as trying to catch all eight members of a set. Oh, the frustration of spotting one only to find at a closer look that it's one of the members you already have!

*Top Row:*
    Baseball Player      $8.00-10.00 ea.
    Dwarfs, Bisque-like      10.00-12.00
*2nd Row:*
    Musicians (Two of Set of Six)      6.00-7.00 ea.
    Figures 2,3,4      8.00-9.00 ea.
*3rd Row:*
    Cherub Musicians, Bisque-like      10.00-12.50 ea.
*4th Row:*
    Baseball Bears (Pink, Blue, Green Colors)      7.00- 7.50 ea.
       Set: Pitcher, Batter, Catcher and Spectator
    Cherub Musician Bud Vases      7.00- 8.00 ea.
*5th Row:*
    Elves, Sets of 6 or 8
       Planter Backs      15.00-20.00 ea.
       Sans Planters      15.00-20.00 ea.

# STATUES . . .

There is not much to say about the next three pages except that they are examples of figurines of this era. All are marked and several have the same base but have been painted differently.

| | |
|---|---|
| *Top Row:* | |
| Ladies | $7.50- 8.50 |
| *2nd Row:* | |
| Lady w/Parasol | 8.00- 9.00 |
| Boy w/Bag | 9.00-10.00 |
| Old Woman w/Balloons | 25.00-30.00 |
| Bullfighter | 8.00-10.00 |
| Boy, Gold and White | 10.00-12.00 |
| *Bottom:* | |
| Lady w/Basket | 8.00- 9.00 |
| Colonial Man | 5.00- 6.00 |
| Last Two Ladies | 6.00- 7.00 |

# STATUES . . .

| | |
|---|---|
| *Top Row:* | |
| All | $6.00- 7.00 |
| *2nd Row:* | |
| 1st and 5th Ladies | 6.00- 7.00 |
| 2nd Lady | 5.00- 6.00 |
| 3rd and 4th | 7.00- 8.00 |
| 6th Lady | 6.00- 7.00 |
| *3rd Row:* | |
| All | 5.00- 6.00 |
| *4th Row:* | |
| 1st Lady Seated | 4.00- 5.00 |
| 2nd and 4th Seated Men | 6.00- 7.00 |
| 3rd Man | 4.50- 5.00 |
| 5th Lady | 4.00- 5.00 |

# AND MORE STATUES

*Top Row:*
| | |
|---|---|
| 1st, 4th, 6th | $6.00- 7.00 ea. |
| 2nd and 5th Lady | 10.00-12.00 |
| 3rd Seated Man | 15.00-17.50 |

*Middle:*
| | |
|---|---|
| 1st Lady | 6.00- 7.00 |
| 2nd Seated Lady | 10.00-12.00 |
| 3rd Lady w/Dog | 10.00-12.00 |

*Bottom:*
| | |
|---|---|
| 1st Gal | 12.50-15.00 |
| Men | 10.00-12.00 ea. |
| 3rd and 5th Ladies | 12.50-15.00 |

# SYMBOLIC FIGURINES

Figurines that are representative of various cultures are pictured here. You can see a pristine Uncle Sam, and Cowboys and Indians of the old West representing the U.S.A. There's a Hawaiian Hula Dancer—of necessity pre-U.S.A.; a turbaned Indian dancer, a Royal Canadian Policeman, a Spanish Matador, etc.

What I want to know is how the grandmotherly-looking Indian in the lower right got to be an incense burner. Now, that would be a story! A little bit of "cultural exchange" going on back then?

*Top Row:*
| | |
|---|---|
| Small Turbaned Boy | $6.00- 7.00 |
| Large Turbaned Boy | 15.00-17.50 |
| Hula Dancer | 10.00-12.00 |

*2nd Row:*
| | |
|---|---|
| Canadian Policeman | 9.00-10.00 |
| Uncle Sam | 30.00-35.00 |
| Large Cowboy | 12.50-15.00 |
| Small Cowboy | 10.00-12.00 |

*3rd Row:*
| | |
|---|---|
| Matador | 8.00-10.00 |
| Cowgirl | 12.50-15.00 |
| Incense Burners | 12.00–15.00 ea. |
| Cowgirl, Right | 10.00-12.00 |

*4th Row:*
| | |
|---|---|
| Indian | 12.50-15.00 |
| Indian in Canoe | 5.00- 6.00 |
| Cowgirl | 12.50-15.00 |
| Indian Incense Burner | 15.00-17.50 |

# UNBELIEVABLE ENDING

When you first spot this picture, you are going to do one of two things. Believe it or not. Now, look closely below the "VI" on the face where it states "Made in Occupied Japan." Not only on the face, but inside on the gears which operate the clock are those collectible words.

I know the history of this clock. It came back with a soldier and had been hanging for twenty years in his mother's basement where she had let it run down rather than listen to it. Well, I oiled it and got it to running and now it hangs in the upstairs hallway of our new home—where it doesn't run as I got tired of hearing the "Cuckoo—Cuckoo" all night. C'est la vie! Anyway, it is a fantastic piece for a collector of "Occupied Japan."

      Clock                                                  $500.00-600.00

# Schroeder's Antiques Price Guide

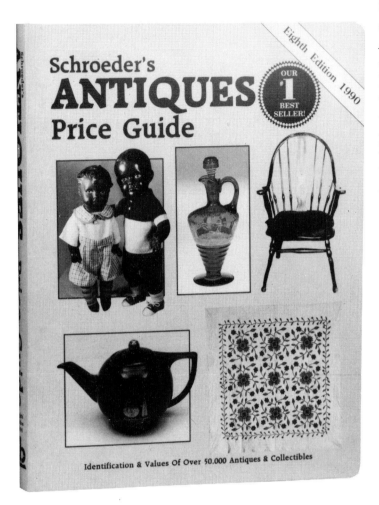

*Schroeder's Antiques Price Guide* has climbed its way to the top in a field already supplied with several well-established publications! The word is out, *Schroeder's Price Guide* is the best buy at any price. Over 500 categories are covered, with more than 50,000 listings. But it's not volume alone that makes Schroeder's the unique guide it is recognized to be. From ABC Plates to Zsolnay, if it merits the interest of today's collector, you'll find it in Schroeder's. Each subject is represented with histories and background information. In addition, hundreds of sharp original photos are used each year to illustrate not only the rare and the unusual, but the everyday "fun-type" collectibles as well -- not postage stamp pictures, but large close-up shots that show important details clearly.

Each edition is completely re-typeset from all new sources. We have not and will not simply change prices in each new edition. All new copy and all new illustrations make Schroeder's THE price guide on antiques and collectibles.

The writing and researching team behind this giant is proportionately large. It is backed by a staff of more than seventy of Collector Books' finest authors, as well as a board of advisors made up of well-known antique authorities and the country's top dealers, all specialists in their fields. Accuracy is their primary aim. Prices are gathered over the entire year previous to publication, from ads and personal contacts. Then each category is thoroughly checked to spot inconsistencies, listings that may not be entirely reflective of actual market dealings, and lines too vague to be of merit.

Only the best of the lot remains for publication. You'll find *Schroeder's Antiques Price Guide* the one to buy for factual information and quality.

No dealer, collector or investor can afford not to own this book. It is available from your favorite bookseller or antiques dealer at the low price of $12.95. If you are unable to find this price guide in your area, it's available from Collector Books, P. O. Box 3009, Paducah, KY 42001 at $12.95 plus $2.00 for postage and handling.

8½ x 11, 608 Pages                                                    $12.95

**COLLECTOR BOOKS**
*A Division of Schroeder Publishing Co., Inc.*